Thames

Steve McAuliffe

Published by Purple Unicorn Media

Copyright © 2016 by Steve McAuliffe

All rights are reserved.
No part of this publication may be reproduced, stored in a retrieval system or transmitted in any form or by any means, electronic, mechanical, photocopying, recording or otherwise, without prior permission of the publisher.

ISBN 9781910718117

Author Photograph by Vicky Slater

Cover photograph from Tyne & Wear Archives & Museums and is used under the Commons license.

Table of Contents

1. Thamesmead
2. Flightless Birds
3. Create Your Own System
4. Return
5. Five Years
6. Awake
7. The Murmurs of Truth
8. Marlow
9. I Am Embedded
10. White Bridge
11. You Are Not These Things
12. We Will Not Remember Them
13. Seven Billion Gods
14. We All Project Upon a Screen
15. The Freedom and Reverie of Words
16. Blood Moon
17. Phoenix Rises, Phoenix Falls
18. The off-duty Frowning Man
19. Redacted
20. Lectured on Morality by Sewer-rats
21. Lord
22. Taking Down Toy-town
23. Thamesmead (condensed)
24. Ta, ta (British Steel)
25. Labyrinth
26. Spanish Practices and an Elephant's Arse
27. Whatever Happened To
28. We who do not look up and they who do not bow down
29. The Parable of the 9 Blind Men
30. Sit and watch the World Turn

THAMESMEAD

I lay amongst the bulrushes
As the ten-hole Doctor Marten boots
Come thundering past
Hoping against hope
That they don't spot their quarry cowering and make hay
With a skinhead moon-stomp upon my face

And though I know this is not the age of miracles
I pray to whatever Cosmic Power dictates the state of play round here:
Sky God
God of the Underworld
Three-headed God
Whoever you are and wherever you reside
Come for me
Now
Take me away and make me safe again
Whispering, whispering prayers into the hard earth -
Praying, praying for two spectral hands to just
Burst up through the soil and dirt
And pull me down
Drag me down
Through the soil
Down through the alluvium
Through the clay
Superficial deposits
And Thanet sands
Pull me through the chalk ridgeway
Down into the middle-third
Down
Down
Until
I merge
Re-emerge from within the inner sun
Like a phoenix re-hatched and reborn
And thereupon
With ten thousand eyes staring intently back at me

I witness Beatrice rapping with Dante
From the seat of a fancy car
Shiny spinning aluminium-plated wheels within wheels
The inferno
Via William Blake
St John of Patmos
And Ezekiel

It's no accident Kubrick filmed his Clockwork Orange Here
A perfect backdrop I suspect for a spot of the old ultra-violence, super-loathing
And mega-fear
And maybe Alex and his droogs gave birth to this shower of shite
Who have me here -
Now
Hiding, cowering in fear
Down in the dirt among the bulrushes
Close to bloody Belvedere

For this is where the hounds of hell
Howl at the moon
As they launch concrete slabs off the roadway bridges
And laugh like coyotes and bitches
As vans and cars swerve into roadside ditches
To avoid the breeze-block doom

Fuck me
Does a sweat-drenched Le Corbusier
Sometimes wake up from his dreaming
-Only to find himself screaming?

Ha, I remember a pompous prick from Surrey once pontificating
At an exhibition dedicated to the Swiss-man's vision.
And I can't quite recall now at the time
If it triggered within me memories
Of the skinhead boots this summer eve
Or maybe another night
When we ran the gamut
Of chasing gangs and lobbed bricks

As we attempted to make our way home
To the relative security
Of our
South
East
London
Suburban
Homes

If I could only
Unlock the secret stone of things
And unleash the power of wonderful workings.
If only –

As behind me the sun sears the concrete ziggurats
The nuclear winter seems inevitable now to all the races
And both the sexes
For Panorama pitched-us our certain doom
And Threads helped sear it further into our cerebral cortex's
And here I am
The Year of our Lord 1983
Somewhere between the dying docks of Woolwich
And dear old Belvedere
This is the place where refugees from the fall of Saigon made their homes
Alongside those evacuated from within the radial blast-zone

And everybody's talking about Thatcherism like its Conservatism on steroids
But for now the brutalist doctrine that the Iron Lady preaches
Has not been linked to the Santiago bleachers
And the neo-liberalism her mentor teaches
Is never betrayed by her grandiose speeches
And how were we to know that Keith Joseph graduated from the Chicago school of Shock and Awe
A decade back in '74
Or thereabouts
It's all swings and roundabouts
And busted bus shelters
You're not alone!

You're not alone!

And anger seems to seep from every pore and bubble-up
Through every crack in every heated paving stone

It's not so much the rivers of blood
But the sewers of hate that
Gush like the forgotten Fleet
Beneath the satellite towns and sink estates

And the inner cities are ablaze these days
Not helped by the cop tightening the thumb-screws
With a sly smile upon his face

And they wonder why we're aimless
Rootless, nihilistic, and dead-eyed
But they do not mention
The seeds of their strategy of tension
To keep us either violent and predatory
Or muted and sedentary
And it seems surely inevitable, even evolutionary
That some evil emissary will cap off this age of Shiva
With the greatest light show the world has ever seen
And will ever see
A fatal inevitable jolt and
All eyes shall be blinded by the flash of Shiva's lightning-bolt

Back up through the sun and strata
The layers of memory and time
The dirt and grime
And I find myself choking on the soil and still red from the inner-sun
Spluttering
Muttering madly
Back into the modernist
Brutalist reality
Of the Thamesmead
Fucking
Estate
And the bulrushes and the here and the now

And the silence
The blessed sacred silence
That speaks of safety
And as I stand and shake the top-soil from my clothes and skin
I feel a change and a charge within
The mushroom cloud duly dissipates
And I swear
I will never surrender again
To a rootless, toothless, shiftless feeling of despair
And I swear
I will not feed the nihilism and fatalism and hate
And I swear
Never again to return to the
Thamesmead
Fucking
Housing
Estate

FLIGHTLESS BIRDS

They tell us we're little more than clockwork meat-machines
And consciousness is just a pre-packed survival tool
But I disagree
I believe
With my night-time aspect
(That is the part of me that dreams and surrenders gratefully to those dreams)
That we are in point of fact
Flightless birds
And our wing-spans
One day will brush the
Very curvatures of space.

CREATE YOUR OWN SYSTEM

Is it just me or does the shit seem to flow one way?
Holy Thursday into Black Friday
And who'll clear out the gutters in your 2.3 million pound terraced house in Peckham Rye?
You know, when push comes to shove.

Maundy Monday and someone let a fart go on the cattle-train transporting us from the suburbs to the processing plants of Old Holborn and Chancery Lane.
The economy took a hit when some geezer hung himself in a tunnel during rush-hour.
He was hoist by his own commuter-belt.

Christ, I must create my own system.
Coz according to the Daily Hate, one in five Muslims now back the caliphate.
And the hate spreads outward,
But the shit still flows one way
Always one way.

Then the City within a city took a bigger hit.
Seems the bankers dry-humped the market too long without mercy, and now everyone's pissing their pants:
Is this the trickle-down effect in actual action?

Listen, William Blake never sheltered from the volcanic ash,
He never holed himself up on the banks of Lake Garda,
Imagination was his salvation – and ours too - if we'd only trace the echoes down through time.
And so we return to Peckham Rye,
Where the angel's perch in the trees
Paying no heed to the
Over-inflated
 Ill-fated
Ever-expanding
 property bubble.

No, there was no Grand Tour for poor old William,
And how was he to know his Arcadian Jerusalem would be appropriated
By fat-faced Tories in their elite drinking clubs up in Oxford?
Those heirs to the Satanic Mills he so abhorred.
They flipped the mills for a profit before the bubble-burst,
And floated mythical Albion on the market
as Jerusalem PLC.
I must, I really must...
I must create something.
Democracy is just a bunch of hand-picked people asking all the wrong questions of all the wrong people –
We are indeed led by the least amongst us. Lions led by donkeys and all that.
And the Mail is getting bolder.
Arab refugees as Mufti's: rats dropping from their foreign robes, scuttling between their smelly sandaled feet.
Swarms and deluges, threatening our identities...
Whilst the heirs to the dark mills sell the power-stations
to the Communist Chinese.
And I tell you what, I'll tell you this –
If that fucking Jeremy Corbyn doesn't prostrate himself next year at the Cenotaph, I'll... I'll fucking...
Ah!
The shit still flows one way and I seriously, I *seriously* need to create my own system and divert the flow, or I will, I will be enslaved by another man's; I will be engulfed by another man's shite.
And when the IRA bombed London, no one blamed the Catholics:
No blacks, no dogs, no Catholics.
They bombed the barracks and the bandstands,
The pubs and the shopping arcades and we stood firm, year upon year: folded our arms, resolute.
We will not talk to terrorists.
And we didn't. One decade turned into another
We will not sit down with terrorists.
Sure enough, we didn't: bomb after bomb = resolute, steadfast.
Then they bombed the City within a City and suddenly everyone's round a fucking table.
Lesson being:

You can drown us in a sea of blood, but don't interrupt the flow of dirty money son.
Ah.
Ash Wednesday as the volcanic clouds that block the sun dissipate.
Trust me now, one more war son, that's all.
And then we'll privatise the fucking lot – one last hurrah.
Chilcot's climbed into his spider-hole for the duration and Blair's on Andrew Marr again – the longest courtship in human history.
Intervention, air-strikes, boots on the ground.
Meanwhile Turkey buys the oil
The oil that funds the bombs that buy the bullets that load the guns that launder the uniforms of the men who drive their Toyota courtesy cars across an air-brushed desert –
Ah fuck this!
-Enough.
Let the lions take down the donkeys.
And let us venerate the Lamb.
Let us re-nationalise Jerusalem,
Here and now, in England's green and pleasant land.

RETURN

It's the things that weigh us down
The petty possessions we pick up along the way
The things we should never pick up along the way
But, hey, that's okay
These things complete us right
At least according to the sons and daughters of the sons and daughters of Edward Bernais
Of course, not everyone can be a nomad
Or a wandering minstrel
Or a holy hermit sat in the city walls
We did however used to believe the mendicant was closer to god
Christ-like in his raggedy rags
And yet condemned to tread the frozen soil for the duration
We believed in the Holy Idiot, devoid of ego and vanity
Condemned to exist in a world of knaves and scoundrels
Despite his lamb-like purity
We cannot change the world by our actions or inactions
But we can perhaps work toward the perfection of ourselves
For perhaps the life lived perfectly is circular after all
It's not the degradation of the material form
But the perfection of the immaterial self, the true self
Perhaps a return to grace is a return to our selves
Shedding clothes along the path of life we eventually return to the source, naked
Best then to know for sure who exactly we are when all is stripped away

FIVE YEARS

Five years it took you mate, mate: five fucking years.
Five years of hoping and praying and waiting and sitting on your fat arse.
-Stretched out on a deckchair you were: watching the apocalypse unfold in miniature, with a tiny drink in your hand.
And you griped and you whinnied:
You bemoaned the death of everything:
How they lost the art of crafting songs:
No longer any bridges and no refrains
And the politicians – all clockwork caricatures for the news crews to dictate to.

But five fucking years mate: while a terrified child was laid out, greyed out: suspended in mid-air.
You just shifted your deck-chair, so you wouldn't rick your neck.
Some neck.
I'm telling you, some fucking neck you got on you mate.

Five years and where were you son?
How could you not have railed against the perversity: the propaganda; the sheer pig-headedness of those wedded to the grand illusion?
And your HD screen was full of life-sized boy-men slathering over barely post-pubescent girls;
And the millionaire footballers with their tattoo's and their Lamborghinis
And by the way, how did the jihadists get all those shiny Toyota trucks? – Who does their immaculate laundry? – And what about the—
-And the ---

You know what: While you watched the horror-show, someone gave it a go:
Yeah, oh yeah: someone tried to change the world, just a little, just a little –
So they shot him down in flames as they do, as they always do.
History no doubt will remember him more fondly,
But history's too late mate, and that's how they like it.

They published a cartoon depicting refugees as rats,

The language of hate, you barely blinked.
You just sat on your hands and determinedly failed to hear the blatant fucking echoes.
The bigger the lie –all it takes –
Good men sitting on their hands as the conductor taps his stick and you stretch back on your deckchair, hands warmed by your fat arse, fingers now entwined behind your head you listen to the silence, counting down:
A-one-and-a-two and a-three –
And here we go:
The show begins.
And the child drops to the ground and the lights dim….
And five years suddenly feels like the beat between a second.

AWAKE

Awake!
So shall we take the path that meanders
Over the aching bridge of Time?
Or shall we simply join the herd
And graze all our life-long days
In pastures enclosed and ever-narrowing?
Should we surrender our dreams
And surrender our souls
And settle for a life that is guided
By an distant brutal hand,
A hand
That assumes the role of God (?)
No.
Christ no.
Listen.
Escape is but in truth return
The narrow confines of the cell-like womb
Cannot
Dictate
The days to follow
See –
Death is not an end
Just as birth is not beginning
Just as Time is not a line
Upon a draughtsman's board.

To transcend this tyranny of Time
Then first my friend, I think we must awaken.

THE MURMURS OF TRUTH

Listen

There is a voice
Just beneath
The constant buzz and hum
It quietly intones just under
The inconsequential chatter
That fills our ears and dulls the senses all our life-long days
Just listen
For it loops a mantra of truth
Relentlessly, over and over
Just out of our carefully adjusted range of frequency
Just turn the dial a little
Because just like Bachelard told us:
The subconscious is ceaselessly murmuring
And it is only by quieting the babble of bullshit and
Listening to those murmurs
That we hear it
In all its simplistic beauty
For it is the eternal truth unfettered and unadorned
And its simple stunning revelation
Will shake the foundations of reality

Just turn the dial a little
Fade out the static interference
And listen

Simply listen.

MARLOW

So he dedicated himself
To the stupidity
And sexual slavery
Of sailors on shore-leave

Whether in the taverns
Or in the knocking shops
Of foul Deptford
He would sniff out their kinks
Like a bloodhound pimp

The Moors, the Spicks, the Arabs and the Chinks:
The international wharf-rats
He'd pick them all clean
Clean as a boson's whistle
Clean as a hollowed out skull

Pity poor old Deptford
He'd sometimes sigh
Ever the poorer neighbour
To Royal Greenwich
Who push their own inconvenient body's forever up-stream

To this cursed place
Where the creator (or re-creator)
Of Tamburlaine
Met his fate
At the point of a stiletto blade

Or was that, as rumours have it
Merely a myth
To mask his spiriting away – under cover of darkness
Straight from the playbook of the School of Night

And as he cradles the dead sailors in his lap

To pull the golden teeth from their crossed-out skulls
Sometimes he pauses
To appreciate the symbolism
Of the moon passing behind the clouds.

And other times he considers
Whether Marlowe's bones do rest
In St. Nick's old charnel house
Mixed in with the bones of paupers
And dead unnamed sailors
And sexual inquisitors
The victims of his own cruel hand
-They who met their fates
In the slimy slipways of the Deptford Docks

And he blesses all their souls
And commits them tenderly to the watery hereafter
Delivers them carefully
Respectfully
 Into the hands of Old Father Thames
For it's nothing personal after all
Merely the dictates of commerce
In this age of trade

I AM EMBEDDED

Sometimes I hear leaves rustling in the basement
Ravens or crows caw-cawing in the belfry
Sometimes I hear
Papers shuffling in a study behind the studded wall
A man once cleared his throat suddenly, abruptly
Before remembering with a barely audible stifled gasp
His task
A commitment to stealthy silence

And sometimes I feel the tug of the puppeteer's strings upon me
Sudden spasms when my shoulders start to sag
And oftentimes my hands jerk involuntarily away from the keyboard
Just as I am poised to share some urgent truth

I am, I fear, an embedded correspondent
Reporting upon my own liberation
Stroke – invasion
Stroke – Occupation
And these soldiers I fear are not my friends
Despite their coarse camaraderie
And rude health
And likewise there is no grand conspiracy
Except that which I orchestrate
And now execute
Daily upon myself

WHITE BRIDGE

They gather once a year
Where the black-robed monks once assembled
In a great gilded hall
There to laugh en masse
At our tax returns
And to guffaw and congratulate themselves
Over great 7-course-banquets.

For hundreds of years they have assembled there
To launch outrageous indignities upon their constituencies
It was here they hatched
The window-tax
The poll-tax
And the bedroom-tax
And on one occasion notable
They held a mock-investiture
And the laughter almost pulled down the rafters
As they ordained the newly-created
Middle-East Peace Envoy

O how their port-stained chins quiver like tasteless shapes
As they regale each other with tales of our hopeless hapless endeavours
And our continued endearing faith
In the rigged but beautiful game

And from time to time they lay down their vintage wines
And abruptly clap their greasy hands
To signal a show of strength for the hoi polio
Thereupon they sit back to watch
The tanks mount the chequered chess boards across the land
And grind the lowly bishops and the lazy pawns
To dust beneath their weighty armoured tracks

See, even though the game is rigged
They still like
To demonstrate from time to time

Their ruthless capacity
To leave no pawn uncrushed

Old Testament in that regard

Yet there is a chink
For none of them can even think
Of the possibility
That any among us here today
Would have the wherewithal and subtlety of thought
To not just step outside the machine
But to create our own machines:
Machines for living, machines for dreaming, machines for flying:
-Let alone weave great ever-morphing systems that create our own realities.
No more Totalities
Thus reducing these dinosaurs to extinction

There is another bridge, not far from the gilded hall
Yet conversely separated by space and time
And there, the ghosts of white-robed monks
Stand before the painted gates
And wait for
Those who have stepped outside
And taken the time
To truly study
A mote of dust
Dancing
In a shaft
Of
Sunlight.

YOU ARE NOT THESE THINGS

Your cherished loyalties and habits do not define you
Your new coat, your phone, your taste in music don't define you
Your newspaper of choice and your corporate coffee house do not define you
Your coat your catchphrase your public laugh, they don't define you
You are not the accumulation of things and practiced mannerisms
Tics and supposed peculiarities
You are not your comfort and your comfortable place
You are not the fat sack you drag behind you
Full of prejudices and responses and endless feedback loops
You are least of all truly you when you set yourself against another
No
You are the spark that only some are privileged to bear witness to
In those moments when your guard is down and your guardians are sleeping
Then and only then outside of your allotted time
In the stolen moment between the second-hand marking down the seconds

When past and future are gloriously suspended
This is when your nature truly breaks through
And you
Break free of the chains of time and mortality's prison
In that moment you are you
And your laughter breaks like a wave across eternity.

WE WILL NOT REMEMBER THEM

We will not remember them
Those unnamed millions,
Those tens of millions
Who died for someone else's Cause
A cause that became a flag to mask the true intention.
We shall not remember they who died for land-grabs
Strategic purposes
or simple geography
Who died for control of trade routes or oil fields or mineral deposits that coursed beneath their naked feet
And you have to wonder: will the blood and bones of the forgotten millions,
Tens of millions
Become over the course of millennia new fossil fuels for men to fight over, to wage war over?
And will those millions, tens of millions of new unfortunates also go unnamed and uncommemorated?
We will not remember them
Then, as now, there will be no newsreaders dulcet tones
Listing their hopes and aspirations
And the hole they left behind in their loved one's lives
We don't wear ribbons or throw buckets of iced water over ourselves to commemorate their passing
Or to wake us from our slumbers
No bugler plays a mournful tune,
No politician bows his brylcreamed head,
No charity depicts the mourning mother carrying her mangled child
No.
At the blooming of the nuclear sun
We will not remember them
At the setting of the same,
We will raise our scarves over our mouths and simply turn away
I have a hunch however that they, the millions, the tens of millions and counting,
They will remember us.
And how will they greet us, at the final count?

SEVEN BILLION GODS

They had me bound up in a straight-jacket of second-hand beliefs
And so I responded to every nudge and poke like a gormless automaton
Different bulbs for different responses
Colour coded symbols
See, somewhere along the line we pissant peasants lost the skill to decode the signs
The wise woman of the village was hung as a witch
So the signs and sigils were surrendered to arch-manipulators
-They who now control the show through fear or superstition-
Playing the old good cop/bad cop routine
Switching roles with the fluidity of Dutch footballers from the 1970's

We were remoulded and rebranded as auto-responders, consummate consumers
The sleeper never dreams he's asleep
Until –
One day, it's like awaking to discover you're still in a dream
In the middle of a maze, in the midst of the matrix
Except it's not you, it's an actor
And it's a film
And the film is classified Fantasy
Though it touches on realities
More profound than documentaries

Hey you! Girl!
No chewing in class
You better listen up coz I'll be testing you on this later!
Come on, move along, next class, next class
Quickly, quickly, no running in the corridors –
Where's your late-slip?
Where's your gym-slip?
Is this your comprehension?
What's all this shit about time-slips?

Look, if school was truly meant to shape us
There'd be classes for day-dreamers
Daily meditation
Not ADD classifications
And mind-chain medications
If they want to teach mathematics, not just numbers in isolation

What about the echoes of eternity?
The golden ratio
The sacred spiral
Thrice great Hermes
Fibonacci sequences
Hell, even Fulcanelli and the mystery of the cathedrals –
Anything is better than this dusty room
And the droning of a tired and tetchy teacher

But in an age of artifice
Price trumps value every time
Just as vitality and sensation
Trump wisdom and contemplation
Everything now has a price
A fire-sale of the vanities
Or the inanities
Less profound than Hollywood frat-boy vulgarities
It's insanity that we surrendered our sovereignty so meekly
And now trade units of our souls for jobs that are supposed to define us
For the duration of our span of usefulness

Vast oceans of creativity course through us
Seas of tranquillity dwell within us
Worm holes to infinite universes are within our grasp
Multi-verses await our attentions at last

And we choose reception as opposed to transmission
Wage-slaves processing whitewash and flannel
Infinity sighs, and seven billion Gods chomp down on pop-corn
In front of the shopping channel

WE ALL PROJECT UPON A SCREEN

A motor idles upon the paved driveway below,
Gloved fingers drumming impatiently upon the cold steering wheel
As in her room she watches her dead idol up on YouTube
It's funny, she muses how no one exists in real time anymore
It seems we are perpetually projecting forward
Or reflecting back
Like a self-aware strip of film.
For ever our time is taken up by anticipation or analysis
And existence is always suspended, temporarily put on hold
Dead air filled with mildly irritating mind muzak
Interspersed with intermittent reminders to hold the line
Hold the line.
And so in our impatience we conjure distractions
In order to lift us out of the moment
For the moment is unbearable, interminable

She tears at a hang-nail with her teeth
As she absently contemplates
Her own absent-mindedness
She returns her attentions momentarily
To the recorded footage of the dead star
To the black star

Even when we return to the now she thinks, we conjure ghosts to reassure us
And the swirling smotes of dust caught in a rigid shaft of sunlight
Seem to project some kind of meaning upon the moment
Something urgent, something bigger, something...
The car horn blasts twice outside
And she is pulled back, re-spooled in effect
She taps a key and freezes the ghost of the dead star
And grabs her jacket from the back of the office chair
And exits hurriedly down the stair, anticipating the admonishment to follow
The chair spins ever slower
Before the frozen screen

And like a projector being turned off
The shaft of light disappears as a cloud breaks the spell
Downstairs the door slams
As upstairs the moment sits suspended.

THE FREEDOM AND REVERIE OF WORDS

The subconscious ceaselessly whispers to you
It whispers
So quieten the world and listen to it telling you,
Prompting you to
Be a wayfarer
A contrarian, to
Wander the earth's surface
In search of your home
But conversely
Not necessarily look up from the book that so engrosses you
Consumes you
But to nurture the freedom
And to ditch your reverence
For the text
For the words are not etched upon stone
But rest upon flimsy paper leafs.
The loose-connecting of isolated words all strung together
Like prayer beads
They weave and bind your freedom
And yet you must permit the words to fly from the page, like sprung angels
Whereupon
You may conjure them into new patterns.

Your reverie
Your harmonic peace
These are the wings of poetry
This is the metaphysics that transcends the razor
And releases
The miracles they told you were manipulations
And the world opens
Your mind opens
Just like a book
As you crack the spine
Break the binding
And unleash at last the age of miracles upon this world

BLOOD MOON

I'm your master set in alabaster
And though my self-aggrandising policies
Are laundered and spun-dry through media machines
There are always certain aspects that require
The old distraction or filibuster schemes
And if resistance hits my purse
And the worse comes to the worse
Then dare you even mention
The tried and trusted strategy of tension?

Ice creams, scream queens, quantum flux-machines
Has-beens, skinny jeans and Judd Apatow's penile-fixated stars of screen
We all agree upon
These hundred million played out scenes.

Distraction is what I need son
Something to take me out myself, you feel me son?
When the day's done
And the sun
Drops like a hot stone behind the boarded-up shop-fronts
And the tired old moon finally drags its lazy arse to light these lazy cunts
Clapped-out wrung out, strung out b-list actors
Clapper-boards and flop-houses, doss-houses
And these swaggering men
Preening like this is their movie
They're all convinced of their own omnificence
Unaware of their own impotence
It's impudent and crass to boot
From branch to root
How these perceivers are little more than receivers
And the masters
Orchestrate disasters
And the wealth of the west is built upon the blood of the east
And the people howl
Howl at the blood-red crescent moon

PHOENIX RISES, PHOENIX FALLS

I still see the glorious currents of confusion
Buzzing and sparking across your baffled eyes,
Like a strip-light shorting, sputtering and flickering
As you try to grasp the scope of the sheer betrayal.
-Bzzz, fzt
And my heart swells with pride
When I witness a copy of the Sun newspaper
Folded upon the dashboard of a builder's van,
The Daily Mail brandished by an immaculately manicured hand.
For I am the Morning Star
Come to guide you down a cul-de-sac
And foreclose on all your dreams.
But first I make you thirst
For your own enslavement,
And fetishize your own entrapment,
To forge your own mental chains
And wall up the doorway to your heavily mortgaged cave.
O but my hearts swells when I witness the division of humanity
Along imagined demarcation lines.
And it fairly bursts with pride
When the greatest shift of wealth is presented as prudence
By my Nazi
Paparazzi
lap-dogs.
Bzz fzt
But you still cannot comprehend, can you my poor, blind child?
-Locked in as you are to your processing plants and your pension plans.
Ever applauding the party-stooges with the finest propaganda served up by own unfair hand.
And yet, despite all this,
Bzz and fzt:
You honour me – ah – with a horse-drawn, ticker-tape parade through your blasted, wasted city.
And I – with mock humility, take the plaudits with aplomb,
Casually, I toss infant livers for my accompanying hounds to chew upon.
Thank you. Again, thank you.

But hear me now, Hope is dangerous naivety
Vision, the province of fools
You, your own judge and jailer,
Building high your prison walls.
Hang on – what's stirring, something – it's amiss ----
Bzzzz Fzzzzz –
Curses!
Like tiny phoenixes the sparks fly upwards as he remembers
The cinders fizz and die as he kicks the fire into fucking embers.
All the traps are sprung as one
The illusions fall like toppled standing stones
The slumbering one awakens
To a system that's now his and his alone.
The street-sweeper cries and
And the blackened church appals
Phoenix rises, phoenix falls.

Agh!
Just like every tyrant down through time,
I showed my hand and fell again
But remember this,
You son of piss
Come morning's dawn
This star will rise again.

Fzzzzzzzzzzzzzzzzzzzzzzzzzzzzzzt

THE OFF-DUTY FROWNING MAN

It's a common sight round here:
The army man
With his service wife towing silently
Two steps behind
Pushing her pram across a sea of eggshells as he,
Furrowed brow marches on grim-faced ahead
Maybe he's trying to get his head around a world without clearly defined guidelines
Or maybe he's angry at the sights he's seen
But I wonder if unbeknownst to him
His anger truly stems
From the surrender of his sovereignty
To a callous, insatiable and indifferent machine

REDACTED

Star-burst fundamental
Entry level number one
Correction
Auto-correction
Log number # 231
Suspected honey-trap
Target best described as louche, unrealistic
This as reported by *REDACTED*
Pronounced limp, a dreamer, doe-eyed and occasionally
Melancholy
These descriptions gleaned from friends and family

Suggestions based on observations:
Rule all passion, faith, tradition
All things tempered with reason
Keep humanity *REDACTED*
Correction
Auto-correction

Faith in State
Faith in couriers and messengers
Carrier-pigeons
Pledge allegiance
Surrender autonomy
Find escape in monatomic gold and Gucci trouser suits
Fun-runs, speculating about off-world civilisations
Ice-bucket challenges and star-gazing
Nude calendars
Talent-shows
The partridge family
And a re-booted sci-fi-franchise

Solidarity with the fallen
Revenge
Prudence
Jurisprudence

Sweaty nights of longing
With a leggy girl from Norway
Hoagy Carmichael
1001 Arabian Nights
Celebrated architects who fill the sky with shards
Digging up the bones of dead archaeologists
Sifting data
Weighing strata in clay deposits
To measure the evolution
Of human consciousness

Mock on Voltaire
Mock on Rousseau

Discussing into the midnight hour
The possibility that the damned create their own hells
And the ignorant their own purgatories
The nameless REDACTED men who plotted to kill a president
Tape-spools
And endless loop-backs
Feedback-loops

Sat within a wall
Listening to or on behalf of fools *REDACT*
Listening to targets deconstructing artifice
In hope of illusory – presumed – salvation
And yet perversely longing
To be part of the conversation
To feel the warmth of
Two minds corresponding
And in time revealing
That within their certainties
In the room beyond this wall
They were in fact constructing a reality
That eliminates the need for walls

Despite the remit
Questions ferment
And bubble to the surface

EXAMPLE:
Why must the touted Age of reason demand the reduction of humanity by eighty per cent?

NOTE:
Last night I dreamt I was Gene Hackman
Tearing up the floor boards
Ripping plaster from the walls with my bare hands
Except unlike The Conversation I wasn't searching for bugs and recording devices
But was trying to claw my way out of a prison

Woke up with fingers bleeding
Unable to re-spool the loops
Sobbing whilst the subject slept soundly
I tore the headphones from my ears
Battered upon the narrowing walls
Frustrated by my inability to gain any purchase
Due to the constriction

Eventually defeated
Crouched in the corner of the crawl-space
Jealous of subject's ignorance
Jealous of subject's innocence
If only he knew I whispered
If only he knew there was a spy behind the curtain
If only he knew that this spy behind the curtain is the insulation in the walls
And if only he knew the answers
So that I may record the answers
If only we all knew the simple truths
That the answer to all questions is
REDACTED

LECTURED ON MORALITY BY SEWER-RATS

The world as it's perceived
-Or as they would have us perceive - is revealed to us
Through an arse-about fucked-up backward screen.
Of course I understand a certain amount of narrative licence must be allowed.
But by Christ they're taking some fucking liberties now.
Political editors plucked straight from Conservative Central casting
Glove puppets or sock puppets - that's our democratic viewing choice.
The bigger the lie and all that...
Listen, we know our politicians are fucking crooked,
But what's up with Andrew Marr's powder-puff interrogations?
And pug-faced Andrew Neil's up in arms about Jeremy fucking Corbyn, again.
This time he's only gone and attended – attended mind you, if you please –
-A Stop the War luncheon.
Hold the fucking press.
See, in this climate, Stop the War is tantamount to a white flag.
And state-sponsored terror is the only reasonable response.

Up yours Delors, you cheese-eating surrender-monkey!
No, none of that, France are our greatest allies now,
Now they've signed-up to the interventionist charter

They're our big old fine old buddies
No mention now of freedom fries or dumping crates of Burgundy
It's shoulder-to-shoulder down the Champs-Élysées
-And wasn't there a bomb in Beirut that killed 46 nameless non-Europeans?

Oi Jeremy fucking Vine –
How much did they pay you to speak at that dinner – dinner mind you, if you don't mind –
How much did the arms-dealers and merchants of death pay you to give them legitimacy? –
-You great lanky streak of paralysed piss.

Finger-in-ear-time
Breaking news: in Amerika one man has single-handedly broken the Bush-Clinton axis.
The everyman, billionaire businessman in the dodgy syrup –
He's the Yankee dream writ large,
-Built an empire from nothing. Well -
His K-K-K craw daddy gave him a million measly bucks in seed money,
Said go and make your fortune son, and he did. Fair play:
He invested it wisely, got the million working for him – in between the bankruptcies –
Eventually built a black pyramid out in the desert/
Coz dying of boredom's worse than dying of thirst.
There's a sign above the door that reads:
'Abandon all Hope ye who Enter – But Empty your Fucking Pockets First'.
America's a nation of rubes, everyone a sucker
Sucker-punched by heavyweight bankers –
'Would you like some out-sourcing on that sir?'
Okay, I know it sounds like a pound-shop soapbox job,
But if you aint got a platform or a stage, what the fuck you gonna do?
Sometimes I convince myself you know,
That the world is waking up, I really do.
But then I see them rushing the doors, grabbing their Daily Fear's
-Clutching their tabloid scare-sheets like fucking crack-pipes.
And then I catch the Politics Show with the career jackdaws
And of course I need to regroup and take pause.
Listen, we could be flying 'pon the wings of poesy.
Not down here, with the Grub Street hacks,
Grubbing around in the gutter,
Flat on our backs in our greasy rain-macs
Taking snaps up the skirts of the muse.

Half the world's in chains
And the other half fears a peasant's revolt.
-Swarms and sand-storms.
And the dreamer awakens to find a nightmare of her own creating.
Whilst the poet, she maintains the dream and still sees the angels in the trees
-And on the corrugated rooftops of the third world slums.

And that is why I will not be lectured on morality by sewer-rats,
Employed on behalf of fat-cats,
Who issue Diktakts via their political middle-men.

Someone said that dreams are collective folk-memories,
Re-interpreted in the unique language of the individual soul,
But being only half-awake and half-asleep,
I guess I could not know.

LORD

Lord, deliver us from this fug
From this mire of myopia
In which we pay for our propaganda
By standing order
Lord
Let us not surrender our libraries
And accident and emergency units
To venture capitalists
And our TV screens to preening propagandists
Who
Causally link anything that smacks of socialism
To terrorism
Or extremism
And warn us not to return to the dark days of the 1970's
(-Although personally music-wise...)
-Whatever, I digress -

Lord
Stop these puppets eliciting Pavlovian responses
By signalling alarm bells
In our carefully conditioned bonces
And Lord,
If indeed thou art singular these days
-For, with all due reverence
I have no particular preference
Who thou art exactly
Old Gods
New Gods
Coalition Gods
And Good Gods
I beseech thee all
(If indeed thee are plural)
To teach me how to find a way
To navigate these murky shark-infested waters
And I know it sounds barmy
But I feel like I should rise above it like a Yogi or a Swami

Simply side-line the fear and hate
And disconnect, meditate
But problem is, I can't delegate
My precious time, see
O great one(s)
And though I would not have the temerity
To presume upon your temperament
I've seen your vengeful nature illustrated in Babylonian texts and the Old Testament
I've read of good men laid low with weeping sores and boils
Rendered powerless to howls and cries
Of their soon-to-be-salt-cellared wives
So I'd guess you have some anger issues
Control issues
And right now, some propaganda concerns of your own
O Great One (s)
But don't you see
With that all seeing eye of yours
That in order to win the public over again to your cause
And win back the faithful
What you need to do My God (s)
Is to create your own media stable
Relegate the once mighty News International
To a modern-day tower of Babel
A New God, laying waste to the Murdoch's and McKenzie's
Taking back control of the manufactured media-stories and feeding frenzies
Manufacturing division and fostering discontent
-And creating belief in a system that profits only you:
The 0000000.1%

TAKING DOWN TOYTOWN (IN THE AGE OF TTIP)

Some of my boys and me
We're going to drive on down to Toytown.
Get us some semblance of redress
Make a pretty mess of their generic
Up-market market-square down there

I'm gonna fire a party-popper up some market-trader's nostril
Let his howls of pain reverberate through the streets, food-banks and homeless hostels
Sally Gunnel, an eight-gallon drum of water and a funnel.
Bradley Cooper in a burning mini-cooper –
That don't compare to what they'll witness down there
After they've encountered me and my super-storm-troopers
Toytown won't know what hit it,
It's gonna brick it.
Little Noddy cop-cars smoking in ditches
A & E packed with rag-dolls in stitches.
The Pew brothers and Barney Magrew on a park bench with a four-pack
Since they scaled down Trumpton's first –response-team due to cut-backs
We're the advance guard, the shock troops for faceless corporations
Small scale doodles this – when we've laid waste to whole nations
And we're gonna lay waste to your precious toy-town
Turn it into another rent-a-ghost-town.
Just like we scalped them all up in Hatty-Town.
Now it's Pound Shops in down-town frown-town.
We left the gollywogs to the ravens
In a forest east of Avon.
We are the emissaries of death and spiritual corruption
We're the shock-troops for nation-state corporations.

Attention, attention:
This is a private sector announcement.
To all survivors present
Please follow the poles with rags that act as marker-flags

And they will guide you to the centre of the market square
For in precisely thirty minutes time from now
Your leader will make a momentous speech from there.
Thereafter food and refreshments will be at hand
Served by our catering unit from the pleasure-park band-stand
And barring any remaining futile resistance
Medical assistance will be available in the forecourt of the old ragged school.

Please do not – repeat – do not make a children's drama from this crisis
This is not the siege of Mafeking or the rise of ISIS
This is merely a reconfiguration, a consolidation
-A natural step toward a one-world conglomeration.
So I say to you, put away your childish things:
We are not your enemies
Put away your wooden planes and your paper-wings
Confine them to your toy-box of infant memories
And finally, to those rusty tin-soldiers holed up in the railway station
I say, lay down your pop-guns, and come and join our federation.
Thank you.

THAMESMEAD (CONDENSED)

Summertime

And the living is sleazy

Boots are stomping

And the tension is high

TA, TA (BRITSH) STEEL

Who'd have thought it, hey?
Although, you know —
Now they told me it makes a horrible kind of sense
And truth be told
Now I'm even more incensed
Than when I first presumed it was just the government
But no
It seems foreign aid's to blame for the closing down of British Steel
For real,
And yes, the Chinese may be flooding the market with their surplus steel
But let's face it,
You have to tip your hard-hat to their entrepreneurial zeal
I mean,
You can see why Gideon got all giddy
When faced with their fearless foreign trade envoys
And why those pesky Tibetans had to be hidden
From sight of the Chinese bullet-proofed conveys.
Jesus,
Even the Queen pumped up the old heraldry
With two days of palm-greasing and pageantry
Boris and David cast as giggling geishas
Blushes flushed their powdered cheeks as they peeked through the azaleas
And now,
Come to think of it
All the U-turns and supposed failures
Could actually all be attributed
To fleeing Syrians
And Libyans
Even Abyssinians
And in general any brown skinned non-Christians

LABYRINTH

We had no choice in experiencing this particular moment in space and time.
We were all rudely called into existence
And immediately thrown into a Minotaur's labyrinth
We've been negotiating the maze ever since.
After 50-odd years of puzzling, I've concluded that the trick
In negotiating an exit route is to separate and rise above, in order to see below
The pattern of endless chambers and cul-de-sacs
-And then in a final coup de grace, to dream the labyrinth out of existence.
The poets and the dreamers urge us to transcend,
To shrug off our rucksacks full of regrets and woes and petty learnt behaviours -
To step out of the wasteland and return to the dream-space of our pre-existences.
Listen, I make no claims: I am not unique, and yet, I am dazzlingly so.
-Just as you are not unique, and yet, you are dazzlingly so.
The same poets and dreamers tell us we're all connected,
And yet conversely untethered from the cosmic mind.
Whilst prominent popular scientists and sceptics tell us we're
Tiny cogs in wheels-within-wheels set in a gigantic and yet finite clockwork universe.
The poet would say they should stick with their material worlds which they can
Weigh and measure, bisect, dissect and quantify.
For the eternal resists the scalpel and the cold razor-edge of reason.
The eternal is unmeasurable, unweighable, un-dissectible and unquantifiable:
-The province of dreams and mysterious consciousness, time-slips and cosmic wanderings.
Thus I conclude we must trust eternity to the poets and the dreamers.
-For it is their songs that dream the song-lines of eternity into existence.

SPANISH PRACTICES AND AN ELEPHANT'S ARSE

I remember one day
A dad of a kid in our class
Came to talk to us about his trade
Proud he was, yes was very proud
Of the trade he plied up on Fleet Street
Closed shop my dad later said
-Closed shop, the Print-
With his usual dismissive sniff
But this kid's dad was very unlike my own
He had the belligerent, unyielding countenance
Of a man used to warming his hands upon the picket-lines
Indeed, it would take a good decade and a half for Murdoch to crush their fierce resistance
But that was all still to come
This man still inhabited a closed-world of hot metal presses, piece-rates and
So-called Spanish Practices
Anyway, he was fierce and proud was the kid's dad
And he worked at the Daily Express
Whose title I recognised well
As it was my grandfather's paper of choice –
Largely for the sport, crossword and cartoons-strips –
(The Gambols never failed to make him chuckle)

Anyway, three decades on I took my Yorkshire wife to Fleet Street
To view, coincidentally, the stunning chromium façade of the Daily Express
And to root out the only London statue to the Virgin Queen
Tucked away and set back from the long paved-over and
Largely forgotten River Fleet

Hidden currents it seems, always churning away below the surface.

When that was done we visited the Old Cheshire Cheese public house
And learned that through the narrowest of alleyways

Some eccentric Victorian once squeezed an Indian elephant
For a bet, or a lark, or a wheeze
Nobody remembers now or cares much anymore.

We sat inside a largely empty bar and imagined what it must have been like
Full of boozy scribes wreathed in tobacco smoke and clothed in sleaze
And printers on double-time, peace-time
Whatever time they fucking fancied truth be told
-All carrying the cocky-certainty of a unionised job for life.
And I thought of my classmate's dad in particular
And I wondered
If alive, does he still bear the scars of the siege of Fortress Wapping?
Does he miss the burning briars?
And the closed shop
The ink-stained fingers
The belligerence
The camaraderie
The firing of the hot presses
The smoky bars
The laughter
The banter

All of which are now like ghosts
Half-remembered like the spirit of class war
Like the statue to Queen Bess and
Like the time they pushed an elephant's arse up a tiny ginnel.

WHATEVER HAPPENED TO...

Whatever
happened
To white dog shit
and sirens that went nee-naw nee-naw.
What became of that?
I guess they went the way of driving gloves and sticky dates that said Eat Me
Grandads who never talked of the horrors of war,
But with eyes displaced
Sat scratching at the frayed covers of their armchairs.
The poppies they wore each November fifth were as much to remember
As to condemn:
The butchery of nations
The wholesale slaughter of men.
Then civilians replaced the armies
As by far the biggest casualties
But we do not remember them.
We do not remember them.
And the poppy became about patriotism and
Those who didn't wear them were spitting in the faces of the dead
The uniformed dead
Whatever happened?
Whatever happened to Magpie and Weeble-wobbles and Mister Men?
Will we remember them or were they a passing phase?
And will we one day remember the phrase Never Again?
-Again.
Look, remembering was once so we wouldn't forget.
It was never merely about the act of remembrance and yet,
We must remember those who lived the horrors, and the horrors themselves.
In order that we won't forget.
And we won't repeat,
We won't repeat.
And we don't let the politicians and the men of state
Take us back to the hell-holes of mechanised carnage.
We will remember them.
But will they forgive us
If we forget why?

WE WHO DO NOT LOOK UP AND THEY WHO DO NOT BOW DOWN

Who embedded this terrible machine within our collective psyche?
And who selected as our cultural intellectual icons
These leaden godless fools
Made heavy and weighed down with solely material concerns?
Is it surely a surprise that mental and spiritual collapse
Continuously rears its ugly head
For those who bow down to nothing?

And nobody mentions the sub-heading of the Origin of Species:
The Preservation of Favoured Races in the Struggle for Life
For it smacks too hard of eugenics I guess
And elitism
And fascism
And every negative ism you could care or dare to mention.

But as always, two false choices prevail:
Original sin or a mere accident of chemistry
Hobson's choice as decreed his Master's Voice.
And how many Christians does it take to cross the road?
-In order to avoid the homeless man in his piss-stained trousers?

No, there must be much more than this and way beyond

For the ghost of man, the magical thinker
Has been seduced and reduced to little more than a pliable piece of spiritual putty
Folded, moulded and sculpted by unseen hands
I look around to see people everywhere standing on their heads
To avoid seeing the world turned upside down
Paying no mind and
Resolutely failing to see that freedom lies
In the nourishment of the earth
And the soul combined.

THE PARABLE OF THE 9 BLIND MEN

I have to say
I enjoy seeing them flailing around
Twisting in the wind
As their narratives come tumbling down
Around their ears
Let it all come down
Let it all fall down I say
Just fan the cards and throw them up into the 7 winds
For all is just illusion anyway
Temporary
Ephemeral
So you may as well just sit on the riverbanks
Silently
Patiently
And wait for the bodies to come floating by

SIT AND WATCH THE WORLD TURN/BURN

I still feel your weasel-words worming through my head
A lack of belief is not a sign of sophistication son
It's an abandonment of the fucking narrative
Flipping burgers like you flip opinions
Swayed, always swayed by prevailing winds
Like an old pervert let loose in the grounds of St Trinian's
You cherry-pick the least offensive sins
And remove your shackles
Only to replace them with manacles
At least Plato's cave-dwellers didn't struggle to pay the mortgage
And sit before the fire paying lip-service to manufactured outrage
And you call yourself free.
Sit and watch the shadows son,
And tell yourself they're real
Sit and watch the sacrifices
And tell yourself you're free.
Sit and bemoan the injustices
And surrender your beliefs
Sit and watch the world turn
Sit and watch the world burn
Sit and tell yourself
Over
And over
You're free
You're free

www.purpleunicornmedia.com

Printed in Great Britain
by Amazon